When Heaven calls your name

People in the Bible who heard God speak

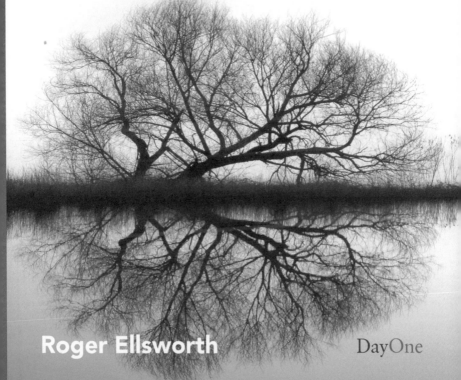

Roger Ellsworth

DayOne

© Day One Publications 2008
First Edition 2008

Unless otherwise indicated, Scripture quotations are from the New King
James Version (NKJV)®. Copyright © 1982 by Thomas Nelson, Inc. Used by
permission. All rights reserved.

British Library Cataloguing in Publication Data available

ISBN 978-1-84625-102-3

Published by Day One Publications
Ryelands Road, Leominster, HR6 8NZ

☎ 01568 613 740
FAX: 01568 611 473
email—sales@dayone.co.uk
web site—www.dayone.co.uk

Designed by Wayne McMaster and printed by Gutenberg Press, Malta

Dedicated to my good friends,
Barry and Brenda Sink

Commendations

*God speaks. He has spoken, and he continues
to speak today. Through these vivid portraits of
Heaven's calls, you will overhear the voice of God
speaking specifically and clearly to you.*

**Todd Brady, Pastor of the First Baptist Church of
Paducah, Kentucky, USA**

*Roger Ellsworth has given us another book full of
pastoral integrity and fidelity to the Word of God. When
Heaven calls your name is both exegetically sound and
devotionally warm—a book that is as heart-stirring as it
is instructional. The readers of this book who hear their
names called will grow in the faith and knowledge of our
Lord and Saviour, Jesus Christ. I heartily recommend it!*

**Ivan Schoen, Pastor, Maranatha Baptist Church,
Poplar Grove, Illinois, USA**

Acknowledgements

I am grateful to my dear wife, Sylvia, for her constant encouragement and capable assistance. I owe a special debt of gratitude to my secretary, Ida Lowery, for her help in preparing these chapters. I further appreciate Jim Holmes for giving me the privilege of publishing with Day One, and Suzanne Mitchell for her very capable assistance in the editing process.

Contents

Introduction

All of God's truths are important, but there are times when we need some truths more urgently than others. The Lord Jesus himself seems to have indicated as much. On some occasions, he prefaced the truth with the words 'verily, verily', which some versions of the Bible translate 'truly, truly'.

There was no shortage of truths for Jesus to share with Nathanael when the two met, but no truth was more crucial for Nathanael at that moment than the testimony of heaven to the nature of Jesus. So Jesus spoke these words: 'Verily, verily, I say unto you, Hereafter ye shall see heaven open, and the angels of God ascending and descending upon the Son of man' (John 1:51, KJV).

We can rest assured that Jesus had all kinds of important truths to share when Nicodemus came to him. But no truth was more vital to this learned Pharisee than his need to be born from above by the Spirit of God (John 3:3,5) and to know that the truth of this spiritual birth was based on the most reliable authority (John 3:11).

The point is that Jesus used repetition to emphasize. We might say he used the words 'verily, verily' to get certain truths to jump up and down and wave their arms at us so we cannot possibly miss them.

The 'verily, verily's of Jesus' ministry made me think about those instances when God the Father or God the Son repeated someone's name. I got to wondering whether those instances of repeated names carried the same meaning or force as the 'verily verily's. Were they intended to make truth dance and cry, 'Look at me!'?

The Bible contains many instances of God the Father or the Lord Jesus Christ calling some individual by name. In Genesis 15:1, we find God saying to Abram, 'Do not be afraid, Abram. I am your shield, your exceedingly great reward.' In 1 Kings 19:9, he inquires of his prophet, 'What are you doing here, Elijah?'

In John 20:16, the Lord Jesus Christ merely speaks Mary's name. In John 20:29, he addresses Thomas: 'Thomas, because you have seen Me, you have believed. Blessed are those who have not seen and yet have believed.'

In John 21, the Lord puts this question to Simon Peter three times: 'Simon, son of Jonah, do you love Me?' (vv. 15–17).

There are, however, only seven instances in the Bible when God the Father or the Lord Jesus addresses an individual by repeating his or her name:

- 'Abraham, Abraham'
- 'Jacob, Jacob'
- 'Moses, Moses'
- 'Samuel, Samuel'
- 'Martha, Martha'
- 'Simon, Simon'
- 'Saul, Saul'

And there is one instance of the Lord Jesus Christ addressing a city in this way: 'Jerusalem, Jerusalem'.

It is always a thing of wonder when God calls any individual by name, but I could not help thinking that the repetition of a particular name signalled something of unusual significance. With that possibility in mind, I examined each of the instances of repeated names. I came away convinced that on each of these occasions, the Father or the Son was dealing with a truth of tremendous importance. I even go so far as to say that these instances give us insight into life's most important and critical issues.

Life is always an extremely challenging business. There are times, however, when it is even more so. We are living in one of those eras. Issues are blurred. Priorities are confused and twisted. Weighty truths are shoved aside and trivial things are elevated.

One of the primary manifestations of the confusion of these days is the assumption that the Bible has nothing to say to us, that something so old could not possibly have meaning for us! But if we have eyes to see, we can find in these instances of repeated names, truths to thrill, guide and comfort.

Sadly enough, Christians, who ought always to be clear-headed and keen-eyed, often appear to be just as muddled and confused as everyone else! Perhaps the God who spoke so emphatically on the occasions we are about to study will be pleased to speak to us through these studies, and will, in doing so, clear our heads and cheer our hearts.

God has one truth in particular that he wants to dance before our eyes—the truth of the gospel. The gospel is the good news that God has done in his Son, Jesus, all that is necessary for sinners to be forgiven of their sins and received into eternal glory. There is no greater truth. How sad it is that it doesn't dance before many eyes!

Because the gospel is so critically significant, it should not surprise us that each instance of God repeating someone's name can be tied to the gospel. We must keep our eyes fixed on this.

And that allows me to say a word about the final chapter. After dealing with those instances when God the Father or God the Son repeated someone's name, I realized that there was yet another instance of a repeated name in Scripture, one which is different from the others. I am referring to that instance when God calls to God. While Jesus, the God-man, was hanging on the cross, he called to his Father, 'Eli, Eli ...' (Matt. 27:46).

That cry, as we shall see, brings us to the very heart of the gospel. I am glad that God has highlighted essential truths for us by repeating the names of certain people. I am especially glad that, on the cross, God called to God in words that believers will never have to use in eternity.

'Abraham, Abraham'

A call to believe greatly in God's great thing

Then they came to the place of which God had told him. And Abraham built an altar there and placed the wood in order; and he bound Isaac his son and laid him on the altar, upon the wood.

And Abraham stretched out his hand and took the knife to slay his son.

But the Angel of the LORD called to him from heaven and said, 'Abraham, Abraham!' So he said, 'Here I am.'

And He said, 'Do not lay your hand on the lad, or do anything to him; for now I know that you fear God, since you have not withheld your son, your only son, from Me.'

Then Abraham lifted his eyes and looked, and there behind him was a ram caught in a thicket by its horns. So Abraham went and took the ram, and offered it up for a burnt offering instead of his son.

And Abraham called the name of the place, The-LORD-Will-Provide; as it is said to this day, 'In the Mount of the LORD it shall be provided.'

Genesis 22:9–14

Abraham was the first man in human history to hear God repeat his name. Abraham was on Mount Moriah to sacrifice his son Isaac when God called to him, 'Abraham, Abraham!' (v. 11).

Abraham was there on Mount Moriah because God had told him to go there. He was there to sacrifice his son because God had told him to do that as well (v. 2).

But God did not for a single moment intend for Isaac to

13

be sacrificed. God did intend to give Abraham a beautiful and compelling picture of the salvation that he, God, would provide through his Son, Jesus. Isaac would be spared, but Jesus would not. We might say that God was intent on making the gospel dance before the eyes of Abraham and Isaac.

God has always had only one plan of salvation. That plan is his Son, the Lord Jesus Christ. People in the Old Testament era were saved as they looked forwards in faith to Christ. We are saved as we look backwards in faith to Christ. Where there is no faith in Christ, there is no salvation.

We like to think that faith is a relatively easy matter and that we are capable of producing it at any time, but faith doesn't reside naturally in human hearts. God must work it into our hearts before it can spring up from them.

Salvation is all of God's grace and that includes even our faith (Eph. 2:8–9). The working hands in salvation are the hands of grace. The receiving hands are the hands of faith.

Throughout the Old Testament era, God was constantly at work to produce, promote, purify and preserve faith.

God had definitely been at work on Abraham's faith. That faith began when God called him back in Genesis 12. Prior to that, Abraham was just another idolater, but that call from God changed his life. That call started him walking with God.

That call revealed that he would play a vital role in God's scheme of redemption. He was to be the father of a new nation, the nation from which the coming Saviour would spring. And the coming of that Saviour would make Abraham's nation a source of blessing to the whole human race. All of this required Abraham to renounce his former life, go to a new land and begin looking forward to that day when God's promise of a Saviour would be fulfilled (Gen. 12:1–3).

Greater faith

In this passage, we find God still working on Abraham's faith by testing it. The Bible explicitly states this in two places. The very first verse of chapter 22 says, 'God tested Abraham.'

The author of Hebrews adds, 'By faith Abraham, when he was tested, offered up Isaac ...' (Heb. 11:17).

Why did God want to test Abraham? Was it to see if he had faith? Such a test was unnecessary. God already knew that faith was there because he had placed it there. The purpose of the test was to make Abraham's faith stronger. Just as the refiner's fire makes a metal stronger, so God sometimes puts his children through the fires of affliction and difficulty to make their faith stronger.

The apostle Peter wrote to suffering Christians, 'In this you greatly rejoice, though now for a little while, if need be, you have been grieved by various trials, that the genuineness of your faith, being much more precious than gold that perishes, though it is tested by fire, may be found to praise, honor, and glory at the revelation of Jesus Christ' (1 Peter 1:6–7).

How did this command to offer up his son Isaac test Abraham? He had had a clear word from God that all his descendants were to come through Isaac. Genesis 21:12 says, '... in Isaac your seed shall be called.'

But Isaac had no children himself. So here was the test: Abraham was called to believe the promise of God that his descendants were to come through Isaac, and still offer Isaac up as a burnt offering.

Two clear words from God, and one word seemingly contradicting the other! What a dilemma! What was Abraham to do? Was he to accept this as evidence that God could not be trusted and refuse to believe either word? Was he to believe one word and refuse to believe the other?

Abraham resolved the dilemma by believing both words from God. He went to the mountain to sacrifice Isaac knowing fully that Isaac had to live. The author of Hebrews says of Abraham, '[He concluded] that God was able to raise him up, even from the dead ...' (Heb. 11:19).

Abraham did not know whether he would actually have to offer Isaac up as a sacrifice. But he knew for sure that Isaac would have to come back down that mountain alive, even if it meant God raising him from the dead. Isaac had to live! God had promised it.

Abraham's confidence that Isaac would live comes out in his words to his servants: 'the lad and I will go yonder and worship, and we will come back to you' (v. 5).

This passage brings us face to face with what faith is, namely, believing what God has said even when it seems foolish to do so.

The passage presents a serious challenge to each unbeliever. The faith exemplified here is exactly what it takes for sinners to be forgiven of their sins.

God clearly tells us that the only way back is through the death of his Son, Jesus Christ, on a cruel Roman cross. What is your response to this? Does it seem to be utter nonsense that eternal salvation can be ours only through the death of a common Jewish rabbi on a cross? Does it seem more likely that salvation comes from merely trying to live a good life? Learn from Abraham, and believe the word of God.

This passage further constitutes a test for each child of God. We live in an age in which the Word of God, the Bible, is mocked and ridiculed. Do we believe it, even though it goes against the wisdom of our age? Or do we find ourselves yielding to the temptation to modify it in order to keep in step with the popular opinions of the day? If we do the latter, we need to learn from Abraham and believe the Word of God, including those parts that are commonly scorned and ridiculed.

God's great thing

Abraham received a great reward for his faith.

When Isaac, who evidently knew nothing about God's command to his father, asked what was to be used for the burnt offering, Abraham replied, 'My son, God will provide for Himself the lamb for a burnt offering' (v. 8).

Just as Abraham was taking the knife in his hand to sacrifice his son, God stopped him and pointed him to a ram that was caught in a thicket, a ram that was to be offered in place of Isaac (v. 13).

With the ram, God not only provided the burnt offering for himself, but he also provided something for Abraham. The author of Hebrews tells us that Abraham received Isaac back as 'a type' (Heb. 11:19, NASB). In other words, this experience was intended by God to be a symbol or representation of something that was still to come, that is, the sacrifice of the Lord Jesus Christ on the cross.

There on that cross, God provided a substitute for all those who believe. Just as the ram took the place of Isaac and died in his stead, so Christ took the place of believing sinners on the cross and died in their stead.

But, in addition to providing something for us on the cross, God also provided something for himself.

What did the cross provide for God? It satisfied his holiness and his justice. You see, God can't just ignore our sin. He is a holy God, and his holiness demands that he judge sin. But God is also a loving, gracious God who takes no delight in punishing the sinner.

We can think of it in this way: God's own nature put him in a dilemma. How could he satisfy at one and the same time his justice and his grace? The former demands that the sinner pays the penalty of eternal destruction and the latter demands that the sinner be forgiven.

The cross is the answer to that enormous question. It was there that God satisfied his justice, in that Jesus Christ actually received an eternity's worth of judgement for sinners. But that same cross also satisfied the demands of God's love, because there is no penalty left for believing sinners to pay. Augustus Toplady has rightly said:

If Thou hast my discharge procured,
And freely in my room endured
The whole of wrath divine;
Payment God cannot twice demand—
First at my bleeding Surety's hand,
And then again at mine.

This account indicates that, in addition to Abraham being given greater understanding of the nature of the coming Saviour's work, he also received the understanding that he was actually standing on the very spot where that work was to be done. The Bible tells us that Abraham called that place 'The-LORD-Will-Provide'.

I don't doubt for one moment that the very mountain on which Abraham and Isaac were standing was none other than Golgotha, and that the site of the altar Abraham built was where the hole was dug for the cross of Jesus.

How Abraham must have rejoiced that day as he and Isaac walked down the mountain together! Abraham had proven again that the word of God is true. But he had also received deeper insight into the work of the Saviour whom God had promised to send.

We can leave this place rejoicing as well if we take to heart the truths so powerfully etched on Abraham's heart that day: the word of God is true, and the work of the Saviour perfectly covers our sins and perfectly satisfies God.

Reflect on these points

1. *Salvation is all of God's grace and that includes even our faith. The working hands in salvation are the hands of grace. The receiving hands are the hands of faith.*

2. *God tells us that the only way back is through the death of his Son, Jesus Christ, on a cruel Roman cross. What is your response to this? Does it seem to be utter nonsense that eternal salvation can be ours only through the death of a common Jewish rabbi on a cross?*

3. *We live in an age in which the Word of God is mocked and ridiculed. Do we believe it, even though it goes against the wisdom of our age? Or do we find ourselves yielding to the temptation to modify it in order to keep in step with the popular opinions of the day?*

4. *God's own nature put him in a dilemma. How could he satisfy at the same time his justice and his grace? The cross is the answer: there God satisfied his justice, in that Jesus Christ received an eternity's worth of judgement for sinners. But that same cross also satisfied the demands of God's love, because there is no penalty left for believing sinners to pay.*

'Jacob, Jacob'

A call to find peace in the Lord[1]

Then God spoke to Israel in the visions of the night, and said, 'Jacob, Jacob!' And he said, 'Here I am.'

So He said, 'I am God, the God of your father; do not fear to go down to Egypt, for I will make of you a great nation there.

I will go down with you to Egypt, and I will also surely bring you up again; and Joseph will put his hand on your eyes.'

Genesis 46:2–4

Jacob, the grandson of Abraham, had twelve sons. He doted in particular on Joseph, the elder son of his beloved Rachel.

Jacob's doting would cost him dearly. It caused the sons of Jacob's other wives to hate Joseph. For a long time the hatred smouldered within these men, but a day came when it burst into flame. When, at his father's request, Joseph went into the fields to check on his brothers, they seized him and sold him to Midianite traders, who, in turn, sold him in Egypt (Gen. 37:1–36).

Through a series of unlikely providences, Joseph rose to prominence in Egypt. Jacob spent years in Canaan thinking that his beloved son was dead. Yet another series of unlikely providences brought Joseph's brothers to the governor of Egypt, where they eventually learned that this powerful man was the brother they had sold long ago. After making his identity known, Joseph commanded that they bring Jacob to Egypt to live out his remaining days (45:9).

Jacob must have been thrilled beyond measure when he learned that Joseph was still alive (45:25–28), but, as the sense of exhilaration faded, Jacob found himself facing a sobering reality. Joseph wanted him to come and settle in Egypt (45:9–11).

This would constitute a mega change for Jacob. He was old. Egypt was very different and, perhaps, dangerous. And Canaan was both his home and the land God had promised to give his descendants. These circumstances made Joseph's proposal seem problematic, to say the least. There certainly was nothing wrong with a visit, but was the settling God's will?

Jacob had determined that he would know the Lord's will about the matter before he left the land of Canaan. He began his journey to Egypt and paused at Beersheba, which was at the very border of the land of Canaan. Beersheba was exceedingly rich in spiritual significance. Jacob's grandfather, Abraham, had called on the Lord there (21:33), and his father, Isaac, had there received confirmation of the Lord's covenant with Abraham (26:23–25). There at Beersheba, while he was engaged in worship, Jacob received the help he needed. There the Lord spoke to him. How often God speaks to his people when they come to him in worship! How often life's problems melt away in the bright glare of hearty worship!

God's personal interest and care (v. 2)

The Lord began his message by calling, 'Jacob, Jacob!' The Lord knew all about Jacob. He knew where he was and what was troubling him.

Many years prior to this, the Lord had given Jacob the name 'Israel', which means 'Prince with God' (32:28). We cannot help but wonder whether the Lord here used the name 'Jacob' as a gentle rebuke for the patriarch allowing himself to be filled with anxiety about the future.

In one sense, we are not at all like Jacob. He occupied a unique place in the economy of God. But, in another way, we are very much like him. We often find ourselves perplexed and anxious about our circumstances and quick to tremble and slow to trust. Let us take consolation from Jacob's experience. Just as the Lord knew his name and his circumstances, so he knows ours. And he feels the same tender concern for us that he felt for Jacob.

It may oftentimes seem that we are not at all important to God. Surrounded by enormous trials and difficulties, we can easily conclude that he takes no notice of us. No less an authority than the Lord Jesus Christ himself assures us that this feeling is not well founded. Our Father in heaven has such an eye for detail that he marks the sparrow's fall. And we are far more important to him than sparrows. He has the very hairs of our heads numbered, and we can be assured that he is concerned about everything that grieves and troubles us (Matt. 6:25–34). How blessed we are to have such a God!

The Lord's words also helped Jacob by reminding him of:

God's perfect faithfulness (v. 3)

After calling Jacob's name, the Lord said, 'I am God, the God of your father ...'

It would have been marvellous enough if God had only said, 'I am God.' By the way, the God of the Bible is the only one who can truly say this. There are plenty of false gods around, but there is only one true God.

If God had added nothing, Jacob would have had cause enough to rejoice. He could have said, 'What a wonder! The only living and true God has spoken to me and called me by name!'

But God also reminded Jacob that he was the God of his father. This brought to Jacob's mind the fact that he and his family were in a special covenant relationship with God. God was the God of Jacob's father, Isaac, because he had also been the God of Isaac's father, Abraham. God had called Abraham out of idolatry and had given him astonishing promises. He, Abraham, would be the father of a new nation into which the Lord Jesus Christ would be born. Abraham would also be the father of a spiritual nation consisting of all those who would put their faith in Christ.

Jacob was part of the covenant the Lord had established with his grandfather, Abraham, and that covenant was still in effect. Jacob was a very flawed man in many ways, but his failures could not negate that covenant. It rested, not on Jacob himself, but rather on God who is always faithful to his promises.

Every believer in Jesus Christ has entered into this covenant. Through Christ, we have forgiveness of sins and eternal life. In the final analysis, it doesn't matter what happens to us in this life. God's covenant precludes any possibility of any real harm coming to us.

We may also assume that the phrase 'the God of your father' caused Jacob to bring to mind the many trials and tribulations his father had experienced. As he thought about these, Jacob had to realize that God had seen his father through much. As Jacob pondered this, he was forced to conclude that the God who had guided and sustained his father would surely guide and sustain him—even in Egypt!

Finally, the Lord's words helped Jacob in that they included:

God's encouraging promises (vv. 3–4)

These verses include four promises:

A GREAT NATION

Firstly, the Lord promised to make a great nation of Jacob's descendants while they were in Egypt. Jacob's settling in Egypt was God's purpose. If he had stayed in Canaan, his family would probably have become absorbed in the Canaanite culture and would never have become a nation. The similarity between Canaanite culture and Jacob's family made this a distinct possibility. But there was no possibility of this in Egypt because the Egyptians themselves loathed shepherds (46:34).

We need only to turn to the first chapter of Exodus to see how completely God fulfilled this promise. There we encounter these words: 'But the children of Israel were fruitful and increased abundantly, multiplied and grew exceedingly mighty; and the land was filled with them' (Exod. 1:7).

So God had it all worked out in advance. Joseph was sold

into slavery in Egypt so that, in due time, God could raise him up as ruler in Egypt and he, Joseph, could then bring all his people there. God is sovereign. His will is never thwarted or circumvented. What appears to be a defeat for him is nothing but one more step on his relentless march to victory.

GOD'S PRESENCE

Secondly, the Lord promised to be present with Jacob in Egypt. He said to Jacob, 'I will go down with you to Egypt ...' (v. 4).

Matthew Henry writes, 'Those that go whither God sends them shall certainly have God with them, and that is enough to secure them wherever they are and to silence their fears; we may safely venture even into Egypt if God go down with us.'[2]

George Lawson adds:

> The chief pleasure of Jacob in the land of Canaan was that God was with him in all his sojournings ... But the presence of God was not confined to the land of promise ... God promised to be with him in the way in which he was now going, and in the country to which he was going. No enemies would be able to destroy him; no accident to deprive him of the possession of his soul; no death to terrify him, if God was with him. We may walk, not only with safety, but with joy, through the valley of the shadow of death if God be with us. Though our heart and our flesh fail us, God will be the strength of our hearts and our portion for ever. How blessed was Jacob, having such a promise as this to

sweeten all his trials! But have not all Christians the same promise to cheer their spirits under every trial?[3]

REMOVAL FROM EGYPT

Thirdly, the Lord promised to bring Jacob out of Egypt (v. 4). This promise included both an individual and a national aspect. The individual aspect was fulfilled when Jacob's sons brought his body back to the land of Canaan for burial (50:12–13). The national aspect was fulfilled when his descendants came out of Egypt under the leadership of Moses.

UNBROKEN FELLOWSHIP

Finally, the Lord promised that Jacob would never again be deprived of Joseph (v. 4). Jacob had been without Joseph for many years. How often his heart ached during those years! But he would never know that ache again. Joseph would be with him all the remaining years of his life and would be there with him when he died. We may wonder why God would promise this to Jacob after depriving him of Joseph's presence for more than twenty years. George Lawson says:

> We must not pretend to penetrate the depth of Divine counsels. God withholds at one time that consolation from His people of which they stood in great need, and at other times gives them an extraordinary measure of consolation. But it would be a great error to suppose that the ways of God are unequal. He always has good reasons for what He does, although He is never bound

to tell us what they are, and does not always, in this world, think fit to inform us.[4]

Bible students have long viewed Joseph as one of the most striking of all the types of Christ. We do well to regard him as such at this particular point. Each believer may rest assured that the Lord Jesus Christ will 'put his hand' on his or her eyes. And when the eyes of that believer open on the other side of death, it will be to see Christ in all his glory.

Life sometimes presents God's people with daunting challenges, just as it did Jacob. But we can face them all with peace if we will remember God's tender concern for his people, his faithfulness to them and his sweet promises. There is, therefore, a sense in which God called all of his children by name when he said, 'Jacob, Jacob!'

Reflect on these points

1. *How often God speaks to his people when they come to him in worship! How often life's problems melt away in the bright glare of hearty worship!*

2. *It may oftentimes seem that we are not important to God. But let us take consolation from Jacob's experience: just as the Lord knew his name and his circumstances, so he knows ours. And he feels the same tender concern for us that he felt for Jacob.*

3. *Every believer in Jesus Christ has entered into God's covenant. Through Christ, we have forgiveness of sins and eternal life. In the final analysis, it doesn't matter*

what happens to us in this life. God's covenant precludes any possibility of any real harm coming to us.

4. *God is sovereign. His will is never thwarted or circumvented.*

'Moses, Moses'

A call to stand in awe of God[1]

Now Moses was tending the flock of Jethro his father-in-law, the priest of Midian. And he led the flock to the back of the desert, and came to Horeb, the mountain of God.

And the Angel of the LORD appeared to him in a flame of fire from the midst of a bush. So he looked, and behold, the bush was burning with fire, but the bush was not consumed.

Then Moses said, 'I will now turn aside and see this great sight, why the bush does not burn.'

So when the LORD saw that he turned aside to look, God called to him from the midst of the bush and said, 'Moses, Moses!'

And he said, 'Here I am.'

Then He said, 'Do not draw near this place. Take your sandals off your feet, for the place where you stand is holy ground.'

Moreover He said, 'I am the God of your father—the God of Abraham, the God of Isaac, and the God of Jacob.' And Moses hid his face, for he was afraid to look upon God.

Exodus 3:1–6

After hearing from the Lord, Jacob did indeed go to Egypt and settle there (Gen. 46:1–28). That settling would prove to have both a positive and a negative side. The positive was that Jacob's descendants greatly increased in number (Exod. 1:7). The negative was that the Egyptians became frightened about the increasing number of Israelites and decided to enslave them (Exod. 1:8–14).

The Israelites would be in Egypt for over 400 years, and most of those would be years of slavery. This was such a difficult and taxing time that many must have wondered whether God had abandoned them, but the years of slavery were all part of God's plan.

God also had another plan: deliverance for his people through Moses.

Although Moses was reared in Pharaoh's house (through another series of unlikely providences!), when we encounter him in the above passage, he seems to be anything but a deliverer. He is not in Egypt but in Midian. There he is not involved in some sort of strategic work, but rather with the tending of the sheep of his father-in-law.

While still in Egypt, Moses had been very zealous for the people of Israel, but he had now been in Midian for forty years (Acts 7:30). He seemed to be on the fast track to nowhere. He may very well have long since concluded that God had no plans for him, that he would live out his days in obscurity. He couldn't have been more wrong.

One day, his shepherding took him to Mount Horeb, which is identified as 'the mountain of God' (v. 1). Mount Horeb was another name for Mount Sinai, which would play such a prominent part in the life of Moses and the people of Israel.

Suddenly, Moses saw something of an eye-popping nature. A bush was burning without being consumed! And God spoke his name from that bush: 'Moses, Moses!' (v. 4).

Moses was destined to see many remarkable things, but he would never see anything more astonishing than this.

The burning bush was not given to Moses just so he could be astonished. It was not given for him to have a sensational experience. Rather, it was given so that he could learn some vital lessons that would sustain him throughout his remaining years. First, the burning bush called Moses to:

Stand in awe of God's greatness

Moses knew about God. He knew that God had called his ancestor Abraham out of idolatry and had made him the father of a new nation, Israel. He knew that God had called Abraham and that nation into a special covenant relationship with himself. He knew that the centrepiece of that relationship was the promise of the coming Messiah. Moses looked forwards in faith to the Messiah.

But while Moses had all this information about God, there was still much for him to know. No one ever knows all there is to know about the true God!

What did this bush reveal about God? It certainly revealed something of his sovereign power. His power was such that he could override the laws of nature, making a bush burn without it perishing.

The bush also revealed something of the self-sufficiency of God. God himself is like that bush. He is never used up with all that he does. His strength is never depleted. His wisdom is never diminished. His grace is never lessened. With all that God has done in the past, he is still fully God. He is sufficient for us as much as he was for Moses and the people of Israel.

The bush also revealed the holy nature of God. As Moses

began to approach, 'the Angel of the LORD appeared to him in a flame of fire from the midst of [the] bush' (v. 2).

We have here a miracle within a miracle. The first is the bush burning without being consumed. The second is the Angel of the LORD appearing in the burning bush.

When we see this term 'the Angel of the LORD', we are probably to understand that the Lord Jesus Christ himself was making what is called 'a pre-incarnate appearance'. In other words, the second person of the Trinity was appearing long before he would actually step into human history in the form of Jesus of Nazareth.

We can well imagine Moses' desire to draw closer to get a better view of this sight (v. 3). But as he drew near, the Angel of the LORD said, 'Do not draw near this place. Take your sandals off your feet, for the place where you stand is holy ground' (v. 5).

God is of such a holy nature that the very ground he touches is made holy, and the slightest particle of dirt from Moses' sandals would contaminate that ground.

The God who appeared here is still holy. He is completely without moral contamination. He is perfect in every way, without any flaw or sin.

What does all this have to do with us? That burning bush speaks to us, even as it did to Moses, about the greatness of our God and the need to reverence him.

No truth is more urgently needed by the church. This is the day of easy and breezy familiarity with God. There seems to be little consciousness of how great God is and how unworthy we are.

Moses would have been well blessed that day if he had learned nothing more than these things. But the bush had more to teach him. It also called him to:

Stand in awe of God's faithfulness

As he stood there staring at the burning bush, Moses could not help but think of his people. They were even at that moment in a furnace of fire in Egypt, a furnace of affliction. But they would not be consumed by it!

The God who was appearing there in the bush also spoke to Moses: 'I have surely seen the oppression of My people who are in Egypt, and have heard their cry because of their taskmasters, for I know their sorrows' (v. 7).

The furnace of affliction could not destroy the people of Israel because God had bound himself to them by covenant. That is the reason he said to Moses, 'I am the God of your father—the God of Abraham, the God of Isaac, and the God of Jacob' (v. 6).

The burning bush urges us to think about God sustaining his people. The church in every age experiences the fires of suffering. Sometimes it seems as if she will cease to exist. We may rest assured that she will not be destroyed, no matter how much she suffers, because the Lord himself is in the midst of her.

We should also apply this on the personal level. The fires of temptation, affliction and difficulty oftentimes burn in the lives of individual Christians, but God has promised that these things cannot destroy us. God will bring each one of his people home to heaven. Not one will be missing.

The burning bush also spoke to Moses at another level, calling him to:

Stand in awe of God's redemptive work

We can find in that bush an anticipation or picture of the Lord Jesus Christ and his redeeming work. I am not necessarily saying that Moses saw this (although I would not be surprised if he did). But looking back at the burning bush from our vantage point, we can see these parallels:

- Just as God stooped to reveal himself in that lowly desert shrub, so the Lord Jesus Christ stooped to take to himself our humanity. Henry Law says of Christ,

  > He is God, and yet He stoops to be made man. He is man, and yet He continues to be God for ever. Withdraw the Godhead, and His blood cannot atone. Withdraw the manhood, and no blood remains. The union gives a Saviour able, and a Saviour meet. Look to the Bush. It shows this very union. The wood denotes the poor and feeble produce of earth ... But it holds God as its inmate.[2]

  Is that not a picture of the incarnation of Christ? He took our feeble humanity and allowed it to hold him as its inmate.

- Just as fire enveloped the bush, so Christ was enveloped by sufferings in his life and in his death.

• Just as the fire could not destroy the bush, so Christ was not destroyed by his sufferings but arose from the grave in triumph over them all.

While God's people can indeed be likened to bushes that burn without being consumed, I must go on to say that there are bushes that will most certainly be consumed (John 15:6). The fires of affliction cannot destroy Christians, because God is with them and within them, but those who have never come to saving faith in Jesus Christ do not have this protection. The most important business in life for the unbeliever, then, is to flee to Christ for salvation while there is still time to do so. Do not be one of those bushes that will be burned in judgement. The Lord Jesus went to the cross for the express purpose of receiving God's judgement in the place of sinners. Take him as your Saviour, and you will never have to fear experiencing God's judgement yourself.

Reflect on these points

1. *God is like that burning bush: he is never used up with all that he does. His strength is never depleted, his wisdom never diminished and his grace never lessened.*

2. *No truth is more urgently needed by the church than that of the greatness of our God and the need to reverence him. This is the day of easy and breezy familiarity with God. There seems to be little consciousness of how great God is and how unworthy we are.*

3. *The church in every age experiences the fires of suffering. Sometimes it seems as if she will cease to exist. But we may rest assured that she will not be destroyed, no matter how much she suffers, because the Lord is in the midst of her.*

4. *God has promised that the fires of temptation, affliction and difficulty cannot destroy us. He will bring each one of his people home to heaven. Not one will be missing.*

5. *The most important business in life for the unbeliever is to flee to Christ for salvation while there is still time. Do not be one of those bushes that will be burned in judgement.*

'Samuel, Samuel'

A call to treasure God's word[1]

And the Lord called Samuel again the third time. So he arose and went to Eli, and said, 'Here I am, for you did call me.' Then Eli perceived that the Lord had called the boy.

Therefore Eli said to Samuel, 'Go, lie down; and it shall be, if He calls you, that you must say, "Speak, Lord, for Your servant hears."' So Samuel went and lay down in his place.

Now the Lord came and stood and called as at other times, 'Samuel! Samuel!' And Samuel answered, 'Speak, for Your servant hears.'

1 Samuel 3:8–10

To get from Moses to Samuel, we must hit the fast-forward button and speed through many years. The people of Israel have been settled in the land of Canaan for more than 200 years.

These should have been good times for the Israelites. They had the Lord God and the good land of Canaan. All that was necessary was for them to order their lives in accordance with God's word and enjoy his blessings.

But these were anything but good times in Israel. Disregard for the ways of God was everywhere, even in the household of the old priest Eli, who was providing leadership for the nation.

Dark times often make it seem as if God is nowhere to be found. But God is always up to something. Just as he had his Joseph to get his people into Egypt and his Moses to get them out again, so he would now have his Samuel to bring godly leadership to the nation.

There was a time when it appeared that there would be no Samuel. His mother Hannah was barren for a long time. But God graciously heard her prayers, and Samuel was born. With a heart brimming with gratitude to God, Hannah took her little boy to live and serve with Eli in the Lord's tabernacle at Shiloh.

The tabernacle was now shut down for the day, and Eli and Samuel had gone to bed. But God was not through conducting business that day. He spoke to Samuel in the night, and, after some initial confusion, Samuel responded and began his prophetic ministry.

In his dealings with Samuel, God was providing his people with something they had sorely lacked and urgently needed—the word of God.

God's word withheld (vv. 1–3)

God has no greater gift to give than his word, and no greater judgement to send than withholding his word.

This chapter begins by telling us that God was withholding his word from Israel: 'And the word of the Lord was rare in those days; there was no widespread revelation' (v. 1).

It was not a matter of there being absolutely no prophecy at all; it was rather that prophecy was very infrequent and sporadic. Chapter 2 mentions a man of God who delivered a prophecy to Eli (vv. 27–36), but that was just one prophecy to one man. A far cry from prophecy flourishing! Ongoing prophecy that spoke to the whole nation was at this point a thing of the past.

How had Israel reached this sad and low state? The answer is ready at hand. The people had stopped listening to God. They had the laws he gave to Moses, and they knew all about the many instances when God had spoken, but they did not prize these things. They had disregarded his laws. They had forgotten the glorious things he had said. Israel was the one nation with a speaking God, but its people were living as if he had not spoken at all.

The very tabernacle in which Eli and Samuel lay down to sleep was a testimony to the fact that God had spoken to Israel, as were 'the lamp of God' and 'the ark of God' (v. 3).

The author's mention of the lamp going out may have been his way of indicating both the lateness of the hour and the immense tragedy of a silent God. When God does not speak, spiritual light flickers and fails!

God's word granted (vv. 4–14)

Suddenly Samuel hears his name called. Old, nearly blind, heavy-set Eli would often have needed help in the night. It is not surprising, therefore, that Samuel assumed it was Eli who called. But, no, it was not Eli (vv. 4–5). The same thing happened a second time (v. 6) and a third (v. 8).

Eli finally realized what was happening. The Lord was speaking to the boy! So Eli sent Samuel back to his bed with instructions. If the Lord spoke again, Samuel was to say, 'Speak, LORD, for Your servant hears' (v. 9).

The Lord did speak again, calling Samuel's name twice, and Samuel responded as he had been instructed (v. 10).

At this point, Samuel was given his first message to declare, one that echoed that which was declared by the aforementioned prophet (2:27–36).

God's word obeyed (vv. 15–21)

Having received this message, Samuel 'lay down until morning' (v. 15). How much he slept we do not know. When day dawned, he would have a solemn task to perform!

He received his opportunity when Eli asked him to reveal what the Lord had said (vv. 16–17).

Samuel's response set the tone for his whole ministry and the standard for all succeeding prophets and preachers: 'Then Samuel told him everything, and hid nothing from him' (v. 18). The apostle Paul so admirably lived up to this standard that he was able to say to the Ephesian elders, '… I have not shunned to declare to you the whole counsel of God' (Acts 20:27).

From that small and faithful beginning, Samuel's prophesying would grow until the entire nation realized 'that Samuel had been established as a prophet of the LORD' (v. 20) and until it touched and nourished the whole nation (4:1). Samuel's ministry was effective only because the Lord 'let none of his words fall to the ground' (v. 19).

Preachers who hold back part of the truth of God in order to ingratiate themselves with their hearers are unworthy of their name and stain their calling.

On the other hand, those who declare God's word in its fullness may take comfort from God letting none of Samuel's words fall to the ground. The same God has promised that his word will not return to him void (Isa. 55:10–11).

What does God's calling of Samuel have to do with us? Why should we concern ourselves with it at all? Interpreters often make the point that God calls today just as he called Samuel so long ago, and that we must be ready to answer his call. It is true—God is a calling God. He calls sinners and grants them spiritual life and faith in his Son. He ever calls his people to greater faith and service. He also calls some to preach the gospel.

But there is a uniqueness about the call of Samuel that we must not miss. The Lord was calling a prophet for himself, one who would declare his word. The fact that he did so at a time when wickedness was so prevalent shows us that God will not allow his word to be overcome by evil. God sustains his own cause. The truth that we should carry away from this passage, therefore, is the indestructibility of God's word.

Centuries later would find many Jews in captivity in Babylon. That would also be a time when evil would appear to be invincibly strong, but those people would find comfort in these words from God: 'The grass withers, the flower fades, but the word of our God stands forever' (Isa. 40:8).

The point at which Samuel's experience speaks so pointedly to us, then, is this: God will sustain and preserve his word. But the fact that God sustains his word does not relieve us of our responsibility. The call of Samuel reminds us that we must be ever eager to receive God's word. John Trapp observes, 'A hearing ear is a sweet mercy: a heavy ear, a grievous judgment ...'[2]

We must, therefore, be constantly on guard against the terrible malady about which the author of Hebrews warned his readers, namely, dullness in hearing God's word (Heb. 5:11). Rather, we must choose to obey the words of the apostle James and be 'swift to hear' (James 1:19).

We must also keep in mind that the primary message of the Word of God, the Bible, is the gospel of Jesus Christ. We cannot heed the Word of God without heeding the gospel it proclaims.

Reflect on these points

1. Dark times often make it seem as if God is nowhere to be found. But God is always up to something.

2. Preachers who hold back part of the truth of God in order to ingratiate themselves with their hearers are unworthy of their name and stain their calling. But those who declare God's word in its fullness may take comfort: God has promised that his word will not return to him void.

3. God is a calling God. He calls sinners and grants them spiritual life and faith in his Son. He ever calls his people to greater faith and service.

4. God sustains his own cause. He will sustain and preserve his word. But this does not relieve us of our responsibility: the call of Samuel reminds us that we must be ever eager to receive God's word.

'Martha, Martha'

A call to settle life's priorities[1]

Now it happened as they went that He entered a certain village; and a certain woman named Martha welcomed Him into her house.

And she had a sister called Mary, who also sat at Jesus' feet and heard His word.

But Martha was distracted with much serving, and she approached Him and said, 'Lord, do You not care that my sister has left me to serve alone? Therefore tell her to help me.'

Jesus answered and said to her, 'Martha, Martha, you are worried and troubled about many things.

But one thing is needed, and Mary has chosen that good part, which will not be taken away from her.'

Luke 10:38–42

We are now centuries removed from the Lord repeating Samuel's name. The Old Testament era has passed away, and the long-awaited Messiah has made his appearance on the stage of human history. Jesus of Nazareth is busily engaged in his ministry of proclaiming the word of God to the multitudes, instructing his disciples, healing the sick and casting out demons—all of which proved that he was nothing less than God in human flesh.

To say Jesus was God in flesh is not to say that his humanity was not real. The marvel of Jesus is that he is fully God and fully man at one and the same time.

As a real human being, he desired the friendship of others, and he had found special friends in Mary, Martha and their brother Lazarus (see John 11).

One of those wonderful times came when it was possible for Jesus to be with his dear friends in their home for a meal. This particular time became the occasion for Jesus to speak a powerful word to Martha.

Martha was not wrong to be concerned about preparing food for Jesus and his disciples. It is certainly legitimate when we have guests in our home to be concerned about their comfort and to provide for their needs.

Yet Jesus rebuked Martha. It was a gentle rebuke, to be sure. We can almost hear Jesus saying, 'Martha, Martha', and we realize that this was no stern denunciation. It was rather a tender rebuke that flowed from genuine concern for Martha herself.

Gentle as it was, it was still a rebuke. And we find ourselves wondering why, if Martha was engaged in something that was legitimate, the rebuke was necessary.

Some try to get around the problem by taking the words 'one thing is needed' (v. 42) to mean that Martha should have prepared only one dish instead of several. But it is obvious from the rest of the verse that the contrast is not between one dish and several, but rather between what Martha chose, serving in the kitchen, and what Mary chose, listening to Jesus (v. 42).

So we are back to the question of why Jesus would rebuke Martha for doing something that was proper and legitimate.

We can only understand why Martha was wrong when we place her actions alongside Mary's. When Jesus began to speak—and the implication is that he began to teach his disciples—Mary began to listen, while Martha continued bustling about with her preparations. Everything had to be just right, and the more Martha worked to make it so, the more agitated she became. Finally, she reached breaking point, stomped into the presence of Jesus and demanded that he rebuke Mary for leaving her. By the way, the fact that Mary had 'left' Martha (v. 40) indicates that Mary had been helping but only stopped assisting when Jesus began teaching. In all likelihood, more than enough food had already been prepared before Jesus even arrived (he did, after all, have a habit of giving people advance notice of his visits—Luke 9:52; 10:1; 22:8).

But Martha could not leave it there. She had to go on and on and on with the preparations until she was exhausted … and angry! So the spirit in which Martha was going about her work was quite as wrong as the work itself.

When, then, do legitimate things become wrong? When we put them above spiritual concerns! By continuing to give herself to her work when the word of God was being taught, Martha fell into the trap of jumbled priorities. She allowed her concern for the good to crowd out concern for the best. She allowed the constant, mundane part of life to eat up what was unique, tremendously significant and swiftly passing—that is, the opportunity to hear Jesus teach. Jesus had come to provide her with a spiritual feast, but she could not receive it because of her preoccupation with her own feast, a feast of temporal things. She was guilty, therefore, of carrying a legitimate concern to an excessive level, and, in doing so, had failed to take advantage of that which was truly crucial.

If we have a tendency to take Martha's side on this occasion, it could very well be because we all too easily see ourselves in her. If we wince at Jesus' rebuke of her, it could very well be because we know that we deserve it ourselves. The truth is that we all have a tendency to engage in 'Martha' living. We are faced time after time with something that is truly crucial alongside something that is passing and ephemeral, and time after time we choose the trivial and carry it to excessive levels.

Much of our happiness in this life rests in avoiding the trap of jumbled priorities, in learning what really counts and living accordingly. It sounds easy, but most of us are finding it to be anything but. We may rest assured that the Spirit of God saw to it that this account was given to us so that we might slip the shackles of 'Martha' living. And we can slip them by keeping in mind three enormously significant principles.

The priority of the Lord

Firstly, the Lord is always to be our priority before everything else. The Lord Jesus allows us no quarter here. When a scribe approached Jesus to ask which is the greatest commandment of all, the Lord Jesus replied in no uncertain terms, '"You shall love the LORD your God with all your heart, with all your soul, and with all your mind." This is the first and great commandment' (Matt. 22:37–38).

Does not your own heart tell you that this is indeed life's priority? Think about it. Your very life is a gift from God.

Your health, your family, your friends, your skills, your possessions—all are gifts from almighty God. James was right to say, 'Every good gift and every perfect gift is from above, and comes down from the Father of lights ...' (James 1:17).

In addition to all of these things, Christians readily confess that the same God has bestowed upon them the greatest of all gifts, the gift of forgiveness of their sins, and that, on that basis, this same God will eventually bring them safely into realms of eternal glory.

In the light of all these things, is it not reasonable to say that the Lord should be our priority? Yet how few professing Christians actually give him that place! How all of us need to hear the rebuke of the Lord: 'But why do you call Me "Lord, Lord," and do not do the things which I say?' (Luke 6:46)!

The priority of the word of God

Giving priority to the Lord means giving his word priority.

The Lord Jesus does not leave it to us to define for ourselves how we should go about this business of giving him priority: he affirms again and again that it is a matter of consistently taking in his words and governing our lives accordingly.

Jesus maintained that his words are so important and vital that one's whole life could be defined in terms of them. His teaching on this point is exceedingly clear. On one occasion, he insisted that the hearing and heeding of his words enables one to be a wise builder who is able to construct a life that is strong and sturdy. Refusing to hear and heed his words makes one a foolish builder who is not able to construct such a life (Matt. 7:24–27; Luke 6:47–49).

He affirmed the priority of his words on another occasion when a woman had fallen into the trap of jumbled priorities. This woman cried to Jesus from the crowd, 'Blessed is the womb that bore You, and the breasts which nursed You!' Jesus responded by saying, 'More than that, blessed are those who hear the word of God and keep it!' (Luke 11:27–28).

When we come to this matter of the hearing and heeding of the words of our Lord, we are dealing with a matter that is at the very core of the life of the church. Her worship services are designed to place the Word of God, the Bible, before us. And here is where the account of Martha really hits home. When we have the opportunity to hear the precious word of our Lord, what do we do with it? If we place the fleeting, trivial concerns of this life—no matter how legitimate they may be in and of themselves—above the hearing of the word of God, we might as well call ourselves 'Martha'!

It doesn't matter whether the concern comes in the shape of a baseball, basketball or football, or in the form of picnics, fishing lures, movies, concerts or television shows; when we put it ahead of the word of God, we have joined Martha in the kitchen. What is the name of your 'kitchen'—that thing, legitimate in its own way, that you use to excuse yourself from hearing and heeding the word of God?

The lasting good

There is yet another principle suggested by this ancient episode, a principle which may be put in this way: giving priority to the word of God produces good that can never be taken away.

We must never forget that the Lord Jesus was not concerned just to rebuke Martha but also to commend Mary. In doing the latter, he explicitly said that Mary had chosen the 'good part', and that he would not take it away from her (v. 42).

Oftentimes, a passage of Scripture contains more than one level of truth. It was certainly so when Caiaphas said that it was necessary for Jesus to die so that the whole nation might not perish. He was speaking about the raw political necessity of getting Jesus out of the way, but, unwittingly, he also proclaimed the central truth of the gospel—that is, that it was necessary for Jesus to die so that others would not perish (John 11:49–52).

I suggest that we can treat the words of Jesus about Mary in the same way. On the surface level, they simply mean that Jesus was refusing to honour Martha's demand. He would not deprive Mary of the privilege of hearing his words by sending her back to the kitchen. But we do no violence to Scripture if we take those words as a picture of an even greater truth, namely, that the words of Christ do good that can never be taken away from those who heed them.

There is, of course, a great day of 'taking away' for all of us. Practically, all the things we hold near and dear in this life are finally going to be taken away from us. Martha's kitchen is going to be closed down. All those things that we have used to excuse ourselves from the word of God will finally perish, but that very word that we so often avoided will be left. The prophet Isaiah says, 'The grass withers, the flower fades, but the word of our God stands forever' (Isa. 40:8).

And on that eternal day, those who have paid much heed to the word of God will be shown to be wise, and those who have not sufficiently heeded it will feel ever so foolish for putting the fleeting, trivial things of this life above that blessed word. May God help us to live now as, on that day, we will wish that we had lived.

Reflect on these points

1. *When do legitimate things become wrong? When we put them above spiritual concerns! We all are faced time after time with something that is truly crucial alongside something that is passing and ephemeral, and time after time we choose the trivial.*

2. *Is it not reasonable to say that the Lord should be our priority? Yet how few professing Christians actually give him that place! How all of us need to hear the rebuke of the Lord: 'But why do you call Me "Lord, Lord," and do not do the things which I say?'!*

3. *When we have the opportunity to hear the precious word of our Lord, what do we do with it? If we place the fleeting concerns of this life above the hearing of the word of God, we might as well call ourselves 'Martha'! What is the name of your 'kitchen'?*

4. *On that eternal day, those who have paid much heed to the word of God will be shown to be wise, and those*

who have not sufficiently heeded it will feel foolish for putting the trivial things of this life above that blessed word.

'Simon, Simon'

A call to rest in the Saviour's care[1]

And the Lord said, 'Simon, Simon! Indeed, Satan has asked for you, that he may sift you as wheat.

But I have prayed for you, that your faith should not fail; and when you have returned to Me, strengthen your brethren.'

But he said to Him, 'Lord, I am ready to go with You, both to prison and to death.'

Then He said, 'I tell you, Peter, the rooster shall not crow this day before you will deny three times that you know Me.'

Luke 22:31–34

It was the night before the Lord Jesus Christ was crucified. What an eventful night it was! The Lord Jesus met with his disciples in the Upper Room, where he washed their feet and instituted the Lord's Supper. There also the disciples had once again argued about which of them was the greatest in the kingdom.

Against that backdrop, the Lord Jesus turned to speak to Simon some very solemn and searching words. We can tell these words were special because the Lord Jesus prefaced them by saying, 'Simon, Simon!' That repetition indicates emphasis.

As we look at the Lord's words, we see that he first emphasized the reality of Satan's sifting.

Satan's sieve

A sieve was an instrument that farmers used to separate chaff from wheat. A farmer would pour his wheat into the sieve, take it into his hands and shake it from side to side. As he did this, the wheat would settle to the bottom and fall through the tiny holes. That which would be left in the sieve was coarse material, which would be dumped and destroyed.

When the farmer shook the sieve, however, the wheat itself would be thrown from side to side. It would be battered.

While the Lord spoke specifically to Simon, he had all his disciples in mind. The first 'you' in verse 31 is plural. The second 'you' is singular and indicates that the Lord was at that point focusing exclusively on Simon, who was mere hours away from denying the Lord Jesus Christ. When Simon later replayed those denials, he 'wept bitterly' (v. 62).

We can well imagine Simon saying to himself, 'Satan did it! He knocked the faith right out of me. He proved that I am chaff and not wheat. If I were wheat, I would not have denied my Lord.'

But on this night, all the disciples of Jesus were about to experience a heart-wrenching time. They were about to experience the battering of Satan. Satan had them in his sieve and he was about to shake them from side to side.

Satan's purpose in shaking and battering the disciples was to knock the faith right out of them. He wanted to show them to be chaff instead of wheat. At the end of the process, he wanted to be able to say something like this to the Lord: 'Here are these disciples whom you have chosen and whom you are planning to elevate to such high positions in the church. Let me tell you, they are more chaff than wheat, and I have proved it by shaking them in my sieve.'

We might say that Satan had asked permission to do with

the disciples what he had done long before with Job. On that occasion, Satan had come to God to suggest that Job was chaff instead of wheat (Job 1:6–12; 2:1–7). The Lord gave Satan permission to put Job in his sieve. The Lord knew that Job was wheat and that Satan's shaking would only confirm it.

Satan did as he was permitted to do. He put Job in his sieve and he shook. How he shook Job! Job lost his family, his health and his possessions. As we read the account, we might very well find ourselves thinking that Satan had indeed succeeded. It often appears that Job's faith is hanging by a mere thread and that that thread is doomed to snap. But when the book ends, Job emerges from Satan's sieve as wheat.

Satan still wants to knock the faith out of God's people and he has all kinds of ways of battering us. He may stir various ones to deride and ridicule our faith. He may point us to the failure of a believer whom we have prized and respected. He may point us to elite unbelievers, the rich, the powerful, the popular, and say, 'You see, these people do not believe in your Christianity. You are out of step.'

He will most certainly point us to our own sins and, on that basis, tell us that we are not true children of God.

Satan has a long memory and, when it comes to sin, he makes sure the believer's memory is also long. Maybe that sin is twenty years old, but Satan still resurrects it and says, 'You see, you are not wheat. You're chaff, and you're not even good chaff at that. You're the worst kind of chaff there is.'

Do we have anything to say to those who are so keenly

aware of being battered and shaken by Satan? Indeed we do. We can tell them that Satan's battering, no matter how harsh it may seem, will not finally be effective. Satan cannot ultimately destroy the faith of any believer in Christ.

Why is this so? The answer is in the second reality of our text:

The Saviour's care

How we should rejoice that the Lord Jesus did not place the outcome of Simon's faith on Simon himself! The Lord took responsibility for his faith.

Jesus did not say to Simon, 'You are going to be shaken by Satan. You had better pray for yourself.'

There is certainly nothing wrong with praying for ourselves when we are battered by Satan, but many saints in Satan's sieve have found themselves so beaten and bruised that they could not pray. All they could do was weep.

Neither did the Lord Jesus tell Simon to get the other disciples to pray for him. There would not have been anything wrong with that, either. But their praying could not begin to compare with the praying of the Lord Jesus, and the Lord here assures Simon that he would be praying for him.

The Lord had already prayed for Simon on that night, and he would pray for him yet again in the Garden of Gethsemane. By the way, the Bible also tells us that Jesus prayed that same night for all his disciples, even future disciples (John 17:6,9,20).

We have a tendency to think that faith is ours to create and sustain. The truth of the matter is that faith is Christ's. He is the giver of it and he is also the sustainer of it. The author of Hebrews calls him 'the author and finisher of our faith' (Heb. 12:2).

While Satan can attack faith and lessen, diminish and reduce it, he can never destroy it. The Lord Jesus himself said, 'My sheep hear My voice, and I know them, and they follow Me. And I give them eternal life, and they shall never perish; neither shall anyone snatch them out of My hand. My Father, who has given them to Me, is greater than all; and no one is able to snatch them out of My Father's hand' (John 10:27–29).

The only way Satan could destroy true faith would be if he were stronger than the Lord Jesus Christ. But he is not. How do we know that Christ is stronger than Satan? Look to that empty grave outside Jerusalem. It testifies that Jesus Christ has authority over all. He has authority over death, hell, the grave and all the tools and devices of Satan.

Here is one way Jesus Christ sustains the faith of his people: he prays for them.

After he rose from the grave, he ascended to the Father in heaven. He is even now at the right hand of God, and there he prays for his people. He makes intercession for them (Heb. 7:25).

What consolation there is in knowing that the Saviour prays for his people! His praying is specific: he knows each of his people and each burden and sorrow he or she bears. His praying is constant: while his people often fail in their praying, he never fails in his. His praying is effective: he will never lose one of his people.

He will bring each one of his children home. Not one will be missing. When we finally come into his presence, we will not say that we are there by virtue of our own wisdom to outwit Satan or our own power to defeat him. Rather, we will triumphantly confess that we are there because the Lord Jesus, who gave us faith, sustained it.

We can, therefore, join John Newton in singing:

> Thro' many dangers, toils and snares,
> I have already come;
> 'Tis grace hath brought me safe thus far,
> And grace will lead me home.

Some good purposes

Most of us find it quite impossible to read the Lord's words to Simon Peter without asking this question: 'Why would the Lord allow his people to be put in Satan's sieve?' He certainly does not have to do so; he is greater than Satan.

We may rest assured that we will never be able to respond to that question to our complete satisfaction in this life, but we can arrive at a couple of answers while we wait for the final answer.

Strengthening faith

One answer is that, by putting them in Satan's sieve, the Lord strengthens the faith of his people. Faith is like gold. Just as gold is refined by fire, so faith is refined by difficulties. It is made stronger and better by hardship.

Strengthening others

Another answer is conveyed to us by these words the Lord Jesus spoke to Simon Peter: 'When you have returned to Me, strengthen your brethren' (v. 32).

The Lord allowed Simon to be battered by Satan so that he would come out of that experience stronger and wiser. And as that stronger, wiser Christian he would, through his writings, prove to be a source of unspeakable blessing to every generation of believers.

One wonders whether this great apostle would have been able to write the following words with clarity and conviction had he not been battered in Satan's sieve:

> Therefore humble yourselves under the mighty hand of God, that He may exalt you in due time, casting all your care upon Him, for He cares for you. Be sober, be vigilant; because your adversary the devil walks about like a roaring lion, seeking whom he may devour. Resist him, steadfast in the faith, knowing that the same sufferings are experienced by your brotherhood in the world. But may the God of all grace, who called us to His eternal glory by Christ Jesus, after you have suffered a while, perfect, establish, strengthen, and settle you. To Him be the glory and the dominion forever and ever. Amen (1 Peter 5:6–11).

Let all who find themselves in Satan's sieve learn from Peter's words. The sieve will never knock the faith out of us, but, in God's good purpose, when we emerge we can help those who are still there.

Do we have anything to say to those who are so keenly aware of being battered and shaken by Satan? Indeed we do. We can tell them that Satan's battering, no matter how harsh it may seem, will not finally be effective. Satan cannot ultimately destroy the faith of any believer in Christ.

The realities of which Jesus spoke to Simon are as much in place today as they were then. Satan is still in the sifting business, and the Lord Jesus still cares for his people. These are not, however, equal realities. Christ's care is far greater than Satan's sieve. Do we doubt the Saviour's care? We need only to look to the cross where he died. If he cared enough for us to go there and receive the wrath that we deserve for our sins, we must never doubt that he still cares for us. If he has already demonstrated the greatest possible care, we can safely conclude that he will not fail to care for us in lesser areas.

Reflect on these points

1. *Satan still wants to knock the faith out of God's people and he has all kinds of ways of battering us. He will most certainly point us to our own sins and tell us that we are not true children of God.*

2. *Satan's battering, no matter how harsh it may seem, will not finally be effective. Satan cannot ultimately destroy the faith of any believer in Christ.*

3. *How do we know that Christ is stronger than Satan? Look to that empty grave outside Jerusalem. It testifies that Jesus Christ has authority over all.*

4. *What consolation there is in knowing that the Saviour prays for his people! His praying is specific, constant and effective: he will never lose one of his people, but will bring each one home.*

5. *The sieve will never knock the faith out of us, but, in God's good purpose, when we emerge we can help those who are still there.*

'Saul,
Saul'

A call to submit to Christ[1]

Then Saul, still breathing threats and murder against the disciples of the Lord, went to the high priest

and asked letters from him to the synagogues of Damascus, so that if he found any who were of the Way, whether men or women, he might bring them bound to Jerusalem.

As he journeyed he came near Damascus, and suddenly a light shone around him from heaven.

Then he fell to the ground, and heard a voice saying to him, 'Saul, Saul, why are you persecuting Me?'

And he said, 'Who are You, Lord?'

Then the Lord said, 'I am Jesus, whom you are persecuting. It is hard for you to kick against the goads.'

So he, trembling and astonished, said, 'Lord, what do You want me to do?'

Then the Lord said to him, 'Arise and go into the city, and you will be told what you must do.'

Acts 9:1–6

This passage brings us to Scripture's last instance of God speaking to someone by repeating his or her name. When we come to this passage, we are only a few months removed from the crucifixion of Jesus of Nazareth.

The religious leaders fondly hoped that putting Jesus to death would soon lead to people forgetting about him. It was not to be. Jerusalem was still in turmoil about Jesus because his disciples kept preaching that he had risen from the grave, and that the resurrection proved him to be God in human flesh.

If there was anything of which Saul of Tarsus was sure, as he rode along the Damascus road under a blazing noonday sun, it was that Jesus of Nazareth was dead and buried somewhere.

It was that 'somewhere' that was causing all the problems. The garden tomb where Jesus' body was placed immediately after the crucifixion was empty. There was no doubt at all about that. The question was, how had it come to be empty? Saul would have none of this resurrection business. As far as he and the other Pharisees were concerned, the tomb was empty because the disciples had managed to skirt all the security, steal the body and hide it.

If he and his friends could just produce the body of Jesus, Saul mused, Christianity would come to a screeching halt. But as it was, the disciples of Jesus were so addled as to believe their own lie, and they were now filling Jerusalem and its environs with their crazy resurrection talk. Still worse, people were believing them. In the few shorts weeks after Pentecost, thousands had come to believe that Jesus was indeed their long-awaited Messiah.

Saul was greatly alarmed because this new sect was threatening everything he held near and dear. He and the other religious leaders had zealously promoted the teaching that one can only reach heaven by earning it through good works, and they had ordered their lives accordingly. But the disciples of Jesus insisted that salvation was not through good works at all, but was rather a gift of God's grace, based on the dying and rising of this man Jesus. The idea that a man crucified in shame on a cross could be the Messiah and the means of salvation was to Saul too ludicrous for words.

It was clear to Saul, then, that something had to be done and done at once. Since they had not been able to find the body of Jesus, the next best thing, as far as he was concerned, was to persecute the disciples of Jesus to the point that they would have more to gain from refraining from preaching their message.

One of the leaders of the Christians, Stephen, had already been stoned (7:54–60), and Saul knew others who were so fanatical that only execution could stop them. But, in his judgement, many could be persuaded to desist from their folly by spending some time in prison.

It was this grim business of executing and imprisoning that had fetched Saul out of Jerusalem and sent him on his way to Damascus (vv. 1–2). Saul was convinced that such stern measures would shortly be successful. After all, why would these people persist in a course that was going to prove so costly over nothing more than a dead body?

Visions of frightened Christians being led away in shackles were dancing in Saul's head as he drew near the city of Damascus. Suddenly, he was dazzled by a burst of light so brilliant that it made sunlight seem like darkness, a flash of light so resplendent that it blinded him and caused him to fall to the ground. While he was writhing in agony in the dust, he heard a voice saying, 'Saul, Saul, why are you persecuting Me?' (v. 4).

What was going on here? Was Saul having a violent

reaction to some medication? Was he, as some have suggested, experiencing some sort of seizure? Had he allowed those he considered to be mad to drive him to madness as well? No; what happened to Saul on the Damascus Road was this: the Lord Jesus Christ intercepted him and brought him to the faith he had set out to destroy!

The evidence Saul encountered

Saul learned that the resurrection of Jesus was not the fanciful imagining of deluded men but was, in fact, an indisputable reality.

After he fell to the ground and heard the voice calling his name, Saul cried, 'Who are You, Lord?' (v. 5). Imagine his surprise when he heard these words: 'I am Jesus, whom you are persecuting' (v. 5).

Although it is not mentioned in this passage, we know that there was more to this experience than Saul simply hearing Jesus speak. He made it clear in later explanations of this experience that he actually saw the risen Jesus (1 Cor. 9:1; 15:8).

This is a crucial point. The voice would, at the most, have proven that the spirit of Jesus was alive, but it would not necessarily have proven that his body had come out of the grave.

Can you imagine what went racing through his mind when he heard those words and saw that form? His first thought must have been that it could not possibly be Jesus of Nazareth, who was dead and buried. But hard on the heels of that thought came another—if Jesus was dead how could he, Paul, be seeing and hearing him?

The conclusions Saul reached

THAT HE HAD BEEN WRONG ABOUT JESUS

It hit Saul at that instant that he had been totally wrong about Jesus. Alexander Maclaren graphically states it: '… the overwhelming conviction was flooded into his soul, that the Jesus whom he had thought of as a blasphemer, falsely alleged to have risen from the dead, lived in heavenly glory, amid celestial brightness too dazzling for human eyes.'[2]

Is it not interesting that Saul saw the risen Lord while he was blind? Up to this point, Saul thought he saw clearly the truth about Jesus, but now, in his blindness, he realized that he had not seen the truth at all. While he was seeing, he was blind; but now that he was blind, he saw.

Many are like Saul of Tarsus. They think that they see clearly on the issue of Christianity. Mention it to them and they waste no time offering their opinions and making their pronouncements. They proudly ride along life's road in supreme confidence that Christianity is all a hoax that has been cleverly perpetrated upon the human race. Despite all the evidence to the contrary, they insist on believing that the body of Jesus is still in that 'somewhere' grave in which the disciples stashed it long ago.

If you are a Saul of Tarsus, filled with yourself and your own opinions, I urge you to please stop long enough to consider the possibility that you might just be wrong. Saul did not think that he was wrong, but he was. And if you deny the resurrection of Christ, you are just as wrong as he. It doesn't matter what most people think about Jesus; even a multitude can be wrong. One thing alone matters, and that is the evidence. Have you ever thoroughly weighed it? Before you pronounce on Christianity, please carefully weigh it. How do you explain the empty tomb? How do you explain the experiences of the hundreds who saw the resurrected Jesus? How do you explain the disciples of Jesus being transformed from frightened cowards into flaming evangelists? An honest and candid appraisal of such evidence yields only one conclusion: that the Lord Jesus Christ arose.

That scepticism hurts those who hold it

Saul discovered that those who deny the resurrection do so to their own hurt.

The living Christ said to the smitten Saul, 'It is hard for you to kick against the goads' (v. 5). The Lord's reference here was to ox-goads, sharp spikes that were fastened to the front of ox-carts. If an ox decided to register his unhappiness about having to pull the cart by kicking at it, those ox-goads would quickly convince him that it was more painful to kick than to pull. Only a dumb ox would keep kicking when each kick brought a painful jab from those spikes.

Up to this point, Saul had been very much like a dumb ox. He had been kicking mightily against the cart of Christianity, thinking with each kick that he was hurting it, but he was in reality only hurting himself.

How did Saul's denial of Christ's resurrection hurt him? The answer is that it put him at war with the very God he professed to serve.

Time after time the Bible tells us that it was God himself who raised Jesus from the dead (1 Cor. 6:14; 15:15; 2 Tim. 1:10). The resurrection was nothing less than God putting his stamp of approval upon the life and death of Jesus and declaring him to be God in human flesh (Rom. 1:4). Saul himself was later to write that Jesus was raised from the dead, that 'in all things He may have the preeminence' (Col. 1:18).

The point is that, if God has invested so much in the life and death of Jesus, it is utter folly for a mere mortal to reject Jesus. Going to war against God simply cuts us off from all hope for the life to come, and it stores up his wrath until it will finally break loose with all its fury on the day of judgement. God is the one with whom we all have to deal, and he will not be kindly disposed to those who have rejected the one he has designated Lord of all. If God has designated Jesus as the bridge from this life to eternal life, a person is a fool if he or she ignores that bridge.

THAT JESUS IS WORTHY OF SERVICE

No sooner had the Lord finished speaking than Saul asked, 'Lord, what do You want me to do?' (v. 6). His question reveals that he had in the space of just a few seconds come to this logical argument: 'If Jesus is risen from the dead, he is Lord. If he is Lord, I am his servant. If I am his servant, I must find out what he expects me to do.'

Such simple and profound logic! It is so simple that it would seem that millions should be asking Saul's question: 'Lord, what do You want me to do?' But, amazingly enough, there are millions who claim to believe in the resurrection of Jesus and yet have not followed the implications of it through to the point of living in obedience to the living Lord.

This, I confess, is a source of amazement to me. I am amazed at those who, in the face of all the evidence, stubbornly refuse to believe in the resurrection of Jesus. But I am even more amazed at those who say they believe it and yet do not have any desire to live for Christ. I can only say that such people have only an intellectual belief in the resurrection and have not truly encountered the living Saviour.

Reflect on these points

1. *Many are like Saul of Tarsus. Despite all the evidence to the contrary, they insist on believing that the body of Jesus is still in that 'somewhere' grave in which the disciples stashed it long ago. If you are a Saul of Tarsus and deny the resurrection of Christ, you are just as wrong as he. An honest appraisal of the evidence yields only one conclusion: that the Lord Jesus Christ arose.*

2. *If God has invested so much in the life and death of Jesus, it is utter folly for a mere mortal to reject Jesus. Going to war against God cuts us off from all hope for the life to come, and it stores up his wrath until it will finally break loose with all its fury on the day of judgement.*

3. *There are millions who claim to believe in the resurrection of Jesus and yet have not followed the implications of it through to the point of living in obedience to the living Lord.*

'Jerusalem, Jerusalem'

A call to consider the cost of rejecting Christ

'O Jerusalem, Jerusalem, the one who kills the prophets and stones those who are sent to her! How often I wanted to gather your children together, as a hen gathers her chicks under her wings, but you were not willing!

See! Your house is left to you desolate;

for I say to you, you shall see Me no more till you say, "Blessed is He who comes in the name of the Lord!"'

Matthew 23:37–39 (see also Luke 13:34–35)

We have looked at the instances when God the Father or God the Son repeated the names of various individuals. We now punch the rewind button to return to the ministry of Jesus and this instance of him repeating the name of the city of Jerusalem. We should, of course, understand that, in addressing Jerusalem, Jesus was addressing its individual inhabitants, and, in fact, all the inhabitants of Israel, of which Jerusalem was the capital.

The Lord Jesus' message to Jerusalem calls us to consider the terrible cost of rejecting Christ's love. Jerusalem had rejected Jesus without realizing the enormity of that rejection. Many are repeating Jerusalem's error.

We cannot contemplate Jerusalem's rejection of Jesus without first marvelling at:

Jerusalem's overwhelming evidence

The people of Jerusalem did not turn their backs on Jesus because they were in doubt about his claims.

It was in Jerusalem that the Lord Jesus said, 'Most assuredly,

I say to you, he who hears My word and believes in Him who sent Me has everlasting life, and shall not come into judgment, but has passed from death into life' (John 5:24).

It was in Jerusalem that the Lord Jesus said, 'If anyone thirsts, let him come to Me and drink. He who believes in Me, as the Scripture has said, out of his heart will flow rivers of living water' (John 7:37–38).

It was in Jerusalem that Jesus said, 'I am the light of the world. He who follows Me shall not walk in darkness, but have the light of life' (John 8:12).

It was in Jerusalem that Jesus said, 'I am the good shepherd. The good shepherd gives His life for the sheep' (John 10:11).

These statements are plain enough. Jesus was claiming to be the giver of spiritual enlightenment and life and the deliverer from God's judgement. He was claiming to be the one and only proper object of faith.

It was one thing for Jesus to make such claims—anyone can make claims! It was quite another thing to back those claims with indisputable evidence. Yet that is exactly what Jesus did.

Jerusalem was the site of some of his most notable miracles. It was there that Jesus healed a man who had been lame for thirty-eight years (John 5:1–9). This healing took place in the presence of many witnesses (John 5:3, 10).

It is striking that the religious leaders of Jerusalem did not question that Jesus had healed the man, but rather quarrelled with him for doing so on the Sabbath (John 5:10–16)!

Later in his Jerusalem ministry, Jesus healed a man who

had been born blind (John 9:1–7). The religious leaders of the city tried to get round the impact of this healing by suggesting that the man had not really been blind (v. 18), but his parents affirmed that this was indeed the case (v. 20).

The leaders then called in the man himself and suggested that his healing had come directly from God without any involvement from Jesus. As far as they were concerned, Jesus was a sinner (because he healed on the Sabbath), and sinners cannot do the work of God (v. 24). Refusing to have any part in such reasoning, this man emphatically declared, 'If this Man were not from God, He could do nothing' (v. 33).

To these two notable miracles we can also add the raising of Lazarus from the dead. Jesus did this in Bethany, which was only two miles from Jerusalem. And he did it after Lazarus had been dead four days and, once again, in the presence of many witnesses (John 11:17–44).

This event certainly caught the attention of the religious leaders in Jerusalem. It wrung from them this admission: '… this Man works many signs' (John 11:47).

The sad thing about these men is that they acknowledged the signs without going in the direction in which those very signs pointed: faith in Jesus.

In addition to the miracles Jesus performed in Jerusalem and its vicinity, we have his authoritative preaching and teaching. These things were of such a nature that some said, 'No man ever spoke like this Man!' (John 7:46).

The most convincing of all evidences would come their way

in Jesus' own resurrection. This compelling event, coupled with the preaching of Jesus' disciples, would indeed cause many to come to faith in Christ (Acts 2:41; 6:7), but most of the leaders and the citizens of Jerusalem, while not lacking evidence for Jesus, rejected it all and rejected him. And the religious leaders planned to kill Jesus, just as their fathers had killed the prophets (Matt. 23:37).

Jerusalem's terrible loss

Rejection of the Lord of glory is no small thing, as Jesus himself makes clear in the words of our text. That rejection would cause two things to befall Jerusalem.

DESTRUCTION OF THE CITY (V. 38)

Jesus says to the city, 'See! Your house is left to you desolate …'

Throughout history, God has used devastating judgements in the temporal realm to picture the far greater judgement that awaits unbelievers in eternity (Luke 13:1–5).

Such a devastating judgement would come to Jerusalem in the form of an enemy invading and destroying her (Luke 19:41–44; 21:20–24). This prophecy was fulfilled with the invasion of the Romans in AD 70.

EVENTUAL ACKNOWLEDGEMENT OF THE TRUTH (V. 39)

Jesus also says, '… I say to you, you shall see Me no more till you say, "Blessed is He who comes in the name of the LORD!"'

This is not a reference to Jesus' triumphal entry into the city of Jerusalem; that had already occurred, and at that time the people chanted, 'Blessed is He who comes in the name of the LORD' (Matt. 21:9).

The people who cried those words did so because they thought that Jesus was going to set up an earthly kingdom. When they learned that he had no intention of doing so, they would cry out, 'Let Him be crucified!' (Matt. 27:22–23).

Jesus was referring, then, to another day when those same people would say these words—the day of his second coming.

The apostle John writes of Christ, 'Behold, He is coming with clouds, and every eye will see Him, even they who pierced Him. And all the tribes of the earth will mourn because of Him' (Rev. 1:7).

At that time every knee shall bow before him and every tongue will confess that he is Lord (Phil. 2:9–11). But acknowledgement of him then will not replace rejection of him now. The apostle Paul says of unbelievers, 'These shall be punished with everlasting destruction from the presence of the Lord and from the glory of His power, when He comes, in that Day, to be glorified in His saints and to be admired among all those who believe ...' (2 Thes. 1:9–10).

Jesus' profound sorrow

Men and women can and do take lightly their rejection of Christ, but he does not take their rejection lightly. He says to Jerusalem, 'How often I wanted to gather your children together, as a hen gathers her chicks under her wings, but you were not willing!' (Matt. 23:37).

Matthew does not specifically say that Jesus wept over the

city on this occasion but, since he had done it before (Luke 19:41), it would not be surprising if he wept again as he spoke these words.

If Jesus did indeed weep, it was because of the immense tragedy of Jerusalem's lostness. He could see the storm of God's wrath coming and, just as a hen uses her wings to shelter her chicks from danger, so he longed to shelter Jerusalem. But while chicks willingly run to the mother hen in times of danger, the people of Jerusalem were unwilling to run to Christ.

The account of Jesus' sorrowing over Jerusalem is in Scripture because it represents realities that are being played out again and again. That reality is this: people are still rejecting Jesus, even though there is enormous evidence for receiving him.

What is the evidence for Jesus? Why should we bow before him and receive him as our Lord and Saviour? The prophecies he fulfilled, the powerful words he spoke, the stunning miracles he performed, his resurrection—all give powerful testimony to the truth of his claims. And all of this evidence has come to us from credible and reliable witnesses.

Sceptics have, of course, tried to overturn the evidence for Jesus, but their efforts have failed. Just as the anvil wears out the hammer, so Christ wears out his sceptics.

Why, then, do so many continue to reject Jesus? It is because the god of this world, Satan, has blinded their minds (2 Cor. 4:4). They do not want the truth to be true, so they turn from it. If they were to acknowledge the truth about Jesus, it would change the way they lived. It would mean breaking with cherished sins and living in a new way. Is there any hope for such people? Yes! The very Lord whom they are rejecting graciously enlightens and changes sinners (2 Cor. 4:6).

Ancient Jerusalem speaks to us about another ongoing reality. It tells us that the very Lord whom sinners reject takes no pleasure in their judgement. He must and will judge all who spurn him, but his delight is in sinners' repentance, not their judgement. The apostle Peter tells us that the Lord is 'not willing that any should perish but that all should come to repentance' (2 Peter 3:9).

In the prophecy of Ezekiel, the Lord himself says, '… I have no pleasure in the death of the wicked, but that the wicked turn from his way and live. Turn, turn from your evil ways! For why should you die, O house of Israel?' (Ezek. 33:11).

If you have rejected Christ up to this point, run to him now. He is ready and willing to receive you. He takes no delight in you perishing, but perish you must and perish you will if you refuse him as your rightful Lord and only Saviour.

Reflect on these points

1. *People still reject Jesus, even though there is enormous evidence for receiving him. And men and women can and do take lightly their rejection of Christ, but he does not take their rejection lightly.*

2. *Why do so many continue to reject Jesus? It is because the god of this world, Satan, has blinded their minds.*

3. *The very Lord whom sinners reject takes no pleasure in their judgement. He must and will judge all who spurn him, but his delight is in sinners' repentance, not their judgement.*

4. *If you have rejected Christ up to this point, run to him now. He is ready and willing to receive you.*

'Eli, Eli'

The call of God to God

Now from the sixth hour until the ninth hour there was darkness over all the land.

And about the ninth hour Jesus cried out with a loud voice, saying, 'Eli, Eli, lama sabachthani?' that is, 'My God, My God, why have You forsaken Me?'

Matthew 27:45–46

We come now to a most fascinating and riveting occasion. In these verses, Jesus calls from the cross where he is dying to his Father in heaven, 'Eli, Eli.'

It is God calling to God!

Jesus was God in human flesh. How can there be any doubt about this? The signature of heaven was all over him the whole time he was on this earth.

- When he was born, shepherds outside Bethlehem found themselves bathed in heavenly light and saw and heard the angels of heaven (Luke 2:8–15).
- When he was a mere twelve years of age, he confounded the scholars as he talked with them in the temple (Luke 2:41–50).
- His earthly ministry brimmed with all kinds of miracles which were witnessed by all kinds of people (John 21:25).
- His teachings were so captivating that some of his hearers were astonished (Matt. 7:28–29; Luke 4:22) and others had to admit that they had never heard such before (John 7:46).

- His disciples, who were closely associated with him and carefully scrutinized him for more than three years, testified that he was God in human flesh (John 1:14).

- He revealed his deity to three of his disciples in a special way when he took on a heavenly appearance before their very eyes (Matt. 17:1–8; Mark 9:2–8; Luke 9:28–36).

- On three occasions, the Father spoke from heaven to confirm that Jesus was his Son in human flesh (Matt. 3:17; 17:5; John 12:27–28).

We need not be in suspense about Jesus. The evidence is overwhelming and convincing. Jesus was the God-man, fully God and fully man at one and the same time.

But, mystery of mysteries and wonder of wonders, this same Jesus is now hanging on a Roman cross! What is God doing on a cross?

The mystery deepens. From the agony of that cross, Jesus cries, 'My God, My God, why have You forsaken Me?'

How can God forsake God? W. Herschel Ford rightly says, 'The crucifixion was the most unusual thing the world ever looked upon—this cry was the most startling utterance of it all.'[1]

Mere hours before he was nailed to the cross, Jesus said to his disciples, '… I am not alone, because the Father is with Me' (John 16:32).

What changed in the space of a few hours? How could Jesus

be assured that God was with him and then convinced that he was not?

The answer to these questions lies in the penalty for sin and the nature of what Jesus was doing on the cross.

The penalty for sin

Human sin is an awesome and undeniable reality. What is sin? It is refusing to live according to God's commandments. It is the creature thumbing his or her nose in the face of the Creator and saying, 'I do not care how you want me to live. I will live the way I want.'

Sin always seems to be the simplest of matters to those who are doing the sinning. As far as they are concerned, it is merely a matter of God turning his head and looking the other way or saying with a shrug, 'Let's just forget it.' Sinners would like for God to be like the indulgent parent who would rather ignore Junior's misdeeds than go through the trauma of dealing with them. Many these days have convinced themselves that this is in fact the way God is!

But the God of our fancies is not the real God. The true God cannot and will not regard sin as a trifling and negligible matter. Why does God take sin so seriously? The answer of the Bible is that he is holy (Exod. 15:11; Lev. 19:2; Deut. 32:4; Josh. 24:19; 1 Sam. 2:2; Isa. 6:3; Matt. 5:48; 1 Peter 1:15; 1 John 1:5; Rev. 4:8; 15:4).

Not only is he free from sin himself, but he also has the deepest aversion to it. The prophet Habakkuk states it graphically when he says to God, 'You are of purer eyes than to behold evil, and cannot look on wickedness' (Hab. 1:13).

God's holy nature requires him to pronounce judgement upon it. For God to ignore sin or refuse to punish it would require him to compromise with sin, and that would make him guilty of sin himself.

The Bible further tells us that this holy God has in fact pronounced sentence upon sinners. That sentence is nowhere stated more clearly than by the apostle Paul in 2 Thessalonians 1:9. There he says of sinners, 'These shall be punished with everlasting destruction from the presence of the Lord and from the glory of His power …'

Note especially that phrase 'from the presence of the Lord'. Sin separates us from God. It separates us from fellowship with God in this life and in the life to come. In Matthew 25:41 we find that God will say to all those who appear before him in their sins, 'Depart from Me, you cursed, into the everlasting fire prepared for the devil and his angels.'

We only have to look at what happened after the first sin in history was committed. Adam and Eve hid themselves from God. They could not stand to be in the presence of the holy God (Gen. 3:8).

The experience of Adam and Eve tells us something else: God does not take delight in punishing sinners. So he came to seek them while they were hiding themselves.

So here is God: his holiness requires him to separate sinners from himself and his grace compels him to forgive those sinners.

The pulsating, throbbing question of the ages, then, is this: How can the holy God both punish sinners and let them go free? To put it another way: How could God satisfy both the demands of his justice and the demands of his grace, when those demands seemed to be conflicting and contradictory?

The nature of what Jesus was doing on the cross

The answer to that question is found in the cross of Christ. Jesus was not an ordinary man dying an ordinary death on that cross. That death on the cross was agreed upon by God the Father, God the Son and God the Holy Spirit before the world began. To be more specific, the three persons of the Godhead agreed that, on the cross, Jesus would receive the wrath of God in the stead of sinners. He would become sin for them. The apostle Paul puts it wonderfully. He says that God 'made' Jesus 'to be sin for us, that we might become the righteousness of God in Him' (2 Cor. 5:21).

Enabled by the Spirit of God to look down the corridor of time and see the cross of Christ, the prophet Isaiah explained it by saying, 'And the LORD has laid on Him the iniquity of us all' (Isa. 53:6).

Now we are in a position to understand Jesus' crying, 'My God, My God, why have You forsaken Me?' Jesus was 'made' sin on the cross. The sins of others were laid on him. And the penalty for sin is separation from God.

For God to count Jesus guilty of the sins of others required him, God, to forsake Jesus, because the penalty for sin is God-forsakenness.

If God had refused to truly forsake Jesus, he could not have counted him the substitute for sinners. That forsaking had to take place!

Some argue that God did not really forsake Jesus on the cross. It was rather a matter of Jesus feeling that he was forsaken. But if it had not been a true forsaking, there would have been no atonement for sinners.

Some explain Jesus' cry by saying that he was merely quoting Psalm 22:1:

> My God, My God, why have You forsaken Me?
> Why are You so far from helping Me,
> And from the words of My groaning?

It is obvious that Jesus was quoting this psalm. But why? The answer is because this verse fits his situation. All of Psalm 22 is in fact a detailed prophecy of his death on the cross. By the way, this psalm also tells us why Jesus was forsaken on the cross, saying to God, 'But You are holy' (v. 3). Jesus was forsaken because God's holiness demanded it.

The glory of it all is that God only requires that the penalty for sin be paid once. If Jesus paid it, there is no penalty left for all those who take refuge in Jesus through faith. In other words, God cannot punish Jesus for my sins and then proceed to punish me as well. That would be unjust! If Jesus bore my God-forsakenness on the cross, there is, therefore, no such forsakenness for me to bear. If Jesus took my hell on the cross, there is no hell left for me, only heaven.

The cross was, then, God's way of satisfying the demands of both his justice and his grace. Justice looked upon the cross that day and said, 'I am satisfied. The penalty of God-forsakenness against sinners has been carried out.'

And grace looked upon that same cross and said, 'I am satisfied. Since Jesus bore the penalty of God-forsakenness for all who believe, they will never have to bear it themselves and can, therefore, be forgiven.'

If someone asks how Jesus could bear in a three-hour period of time an eternity's worth of wrath, we must admit that we are out of our element. We can only say that, as God in human flesh, Jesus had the capacity to bear an infinite amount of wrath in a finite amount of time. What a wonder!

It is noteworthy that nature itself gave testimony to the reality of Jesus being forsaken by God.

Jesus was nailed to the cross at nine in the morning. He died at three in the afternoon. From noon until three, darkness fell over the land, the hours at which the sun normally shines its brightest. These hours were, in the words of William Hendriksen, 'intense and unforgettable'.[2]

Thomas Manton says, 'The sun seemed to be struck blind with astonishment, and the frame of nature to put itself into a funeral garb and habit, as if the creatures durst not show their glory while ... Christ was suffering.'[3]

Perhaps Charles Spurgeon put it best: 'It was midnight at midday.'[4]

Never has there been such darkness. When Jesus was born, a brilliant burst of light bathed the fields around Bethlehem (Luke 2:9), but at his death there was no light but only the deepest darkness.

After those three long hours of darkness, Jesus cried, 'My God, My God, why have You forsaken Me?'

This is the fourth word from the cross with three words on each side of it. It is, therefore, the centre word, and that is singularly appropriate, because it brings us to the very centre of what Jesus' death was all about. This was Jesus' own explanation of those hours of darkness. They were hours in which God withdrew from him and turned his back on him. During these hours Jesus was deprived of fellowship and communion with God.

Now we can understand why a thick veil of darkness was drawn around the land at the time of the crucifixion. It was a visible and outward manifestation of God's withdrawal from Jesus. The Bible says, 'God is light' (1 John 1:5). So if God withdrew from Jesus, darkness would be fitting.

We do not appropriately handle Jesus' wail to his Father if we do not drill our hearts in the wonder of it. Jesus, who lived his whole life in communion with the Father, was separated from him. And the thing that should continually amaze and astound us is that he bore it all for undeserving sinners. Because

Jesus cried, 'My God, My God, why have You forsaken Me?',
those who believe in him will not have to cry it in eternity.

> His body broken, nail'd, and torn,
> And stain'd with streams of blood,
> His spotless soul was left forlorn,
> Forsaken of his God.
>
> 'Twas then his Father gave the stroke,
> That justice did decree;
> All nature felt the dreadful stroke,
> When Jesus died for me.
>
> Eli lama sabachthani,
> My God, my God, he cried,
> Why hast thou thus forsaken me!
> And thus my Saviour died.
>
> But why did God forsake his Son,
> When bleeding on the tree?
> He died for sins, but not his own,
> For Jesus died for me.
>
> My guilt was on my Surety laid
> And therefore he must die;
> His soul a sacrifice was made
> For such a worm as I.

Was ever love so great as this?
Was ever grace so free?
This is my glory, joy and bliss,
That Jesus died for me.

(author unknown)

Let us know beyond any shadow of doubt that God will either find our sins on Jesus or on us. If he finds them on Jesus, we will never have to endure their penalty, but if he finds them on us, we must hear from God those tragic words: 'Depart from Me.'

W. Herschel Ford pointedly writes:

God spared not the Lord Jesus when He found sin on Him—the sin of others. Do you think He will spare you if you come up to judgment with your own sin on you? If He poured out His wrath on Him who bore no sin but ours, do you think He will hold back His wrath if you go on in sin and come to the end of the way with your sin still on you? But there is hope for you. 'He that believeth on the Son hath life, but he that believeth not the Son shall not see life, but the wrath of God abideth on him.'[5]

Reflect on these points

1. God's holy nature requires him to pronounce judgement upon sin. For God to ignore it or refuse to punish it would require him to compromise with sin, and that would make him guilty of sin himself.

2. *God's holiness requires him to separate sinners from himself and his grace compels him to forgive those sinners.*

3. *For God to count Jesus guilty of the sins of others required him, God, to forsake Jesus, because the penalty for sin is God-forsakenness. If he had refused to truly forsake Jesus, he could not have counted him the substitute for sinners. That forsaking had to take place!*

4. *Jesus, who lived his whole life in communion with the Father, was separated from him. And he bore it all for undeserving sinners.*

5. *God only requires that the penalty for sin be paid once. If Jesus paid it, there is no penalty left for all those who take refuge in Jesus through faith. God cannot punish Jesus for my sins and then proceed to punish me as well. That would be unjust! If Jesus took my hell on the cross, there is no hell left for me, only heaven.*

Endnotes

'Jacob, Jacob'

1 A similar chapter can be found in my book *Be Patient: God Hasn't Finished with Me Yet!* (Darlington: Evangelical Press, 2003), pp. 95–100.

2 Matthew Henry, *Matthew Henry's Commentary*, vol. I ((n.p.) Fleming H. Revell (n.d.)), p. 248.

3 George Lawson, *The Life of Joseph* (Edinburgh: Banner of Truth, 1988), p. 313.

4 Ibid., p. 316.

'Moses, Moses'

1 A similar chapter can be found in my book *Moses: God's Man for Challenging Times* (Darlington: Evangelical Press, 2005), pp. 31–35.

2 Henry Law, *The Gospel in Exodus* (London: Banner of Truth, 1967), pp. 9–10.

'Samuel, Samuel'

1 A similar chapter appears in my book *Face2Face with Samuel: Encountering Samuel the King-Maker* (Leominster: Day One, 2006), pp. 29–34.

2 John Trapp, *Commentary on the Old & New Testaments*, vol. i (Eureka, CA: Tanski Publications, 1997), p. 418.

'Martha, Martha'

1 A similar chapter can be found in my book *How to Live in a Dangerous World* (Darlington: Evangelical Press, 1998), pp. 205–10.

'Simon, Simon'

1 A similar chapter can be found in my book *Christian Comfort* (Darlington: Evangelical Press, 2003), pp. 182–91.

'Saul, Saul'

1 A similar chapter can be found in my book *How to Live in a Dangerous World*, pp. 122–127.

2 Alexander Maclaren, *Expositions of Holy Scripture*, vol. xi (Grand Rapids, MI: Baker Book House, 1974), p. 265.

'Eli, Eli'

1 W. Herschel Ford, *Seven Simple Sermons on the Saviour's Last Words* (Grand Rapids, MI: Zondervan, 1953), p. 46.

2 William Hendriksen, *New Testament Commentary: Luke* (Grand Rapids, MI: Baker Book House, 1978), p. 1034.

3 Thomas Manton, *The Complete Works of Thomas Manton*, vol. ii (Worthington, PA: Maranatha Publications (n.d.)), p. 265.

4 Quoted by A.W. Pink, *The Seven Sayings of the Saviour on the Cross* (Grand Rapids, MI: Baker Book House, 1984), p. 79.

5 Ford, *Seven Simple Sermons*, pp. 55–56.

ABOUT DAY ONE:

Day One's threefold commitment:

- To be faithful to the Bible, God's inerrant, infallible Word;
- To be relevant to our modern generation;
- To be excellent in our publication standards.

I continue to be thankful for the publications of Day One. They are biblical; they have sound theology; and they are relevant to the issues at hand. The material is condensed and manageable while, at the same time, being complete—a challenging balance to find. We are happy in our ministry to make use of these excellent publications.

JOHN MACARTHUR, PASTOR-TEACHER, GRACE COMMUNITY CHURCH, CALIFORNIA

It is a great encouragement to see Day One making such excellent progress. Their publications are always biblical, accessible and attractively produced, with no compromise on quality. Long may their progress continue and increase!

JOHN BLANCHARD, AUTHOR, EVANGELIST AND APOLOGIST

Visit our web site for more information and
to request a free catalogue of our books.

www.dayone.co.uk

They echoed the voice of God

Reflections on the Minor Prophets

ROGER ELLSWORTH

128PP, PAPERBACK

ISBN 978-1-84625-101-6

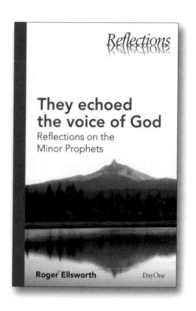

Many carry a little Bible and believe in a little God. Their Bibles are little because they ignore so many of its books. Their God is little because they ignore so many of the Bible's truths. The Minor Prophets can help us. These men made sense of their circumstances and found strength for their challenges by basking in the God who was above it all and in it all. The God they served was wise enough to plan and strong enough to achieve. This study of their messages will help us have both bigger Bibles and a bigger God.

'Roger Ellsworth helps us appreciate how the so-called Minor Prophets make known the character and work of our great God. This book is a great introduction to and overview of their prophecies. Read it to become acquainted with these sometimes overlooked servants and, more importantly, with the unchangeable God whose message they proclaimed.'
TOM ASCOL, DIRECTOR OF FOUNDERS MINISTRIES AND PASTOR, GRACE BAPTIST CHURCH, CAPE CORAL, FLORIDA

'Laced with helpful, practical application, this book shows how each prophet emphasized a particular aspect of God's character, giving an overall picture that is compelling.'
JIM WINTER, MINISTER OF HORSELL EVANGELICAL CHURCH, WOKING, ENGLAND

Under God's smile

The Trinitarian Blessing of
2 Corinthians 13:14

DEREK PRIME

128PP, PAPERBACK

ISBN 978-1-84625-059-0

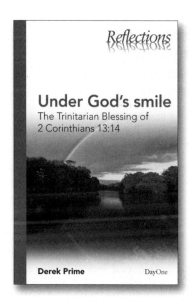

During recent decades, it has become the practice of Christians in many churches and in university and college Christian Unions to commit one another to God's grace and care with the words 'May the grace of the Lord Jesus Christ, and the love of God, and the fellowship of the Holy Spirit be with us all' (2 Corinthians 13:14). They are familiar words, but what do they actually mean? For what are we praying?

So that we do not repeat these words without appreciating their full implication, Derek Prime explores them and considers the three Persons of the Trinity in their different, yet perfectly harmonious, relationship to every believer. Written in an easy-to-read style, this book is thoroughly rooted in the Scriptures and is a demonstration that solid biblical truth is both heart-warming and exciting.

'Wholesome food for the average Christian reader and devotional writing of the highest order'
EVANGELICALS NOW

'An easily-read book, helpful in all stages of Christian life'
GRACE MAGAZINE

'Derek Prime's ministry is much appreciated by many Christian groups, including ourselves. Like all his other books … biblically based and easy to read'
ASSOCIATED PRESBYTERIANS NEWS

'If, like me, you are constantly on the lookout for books that say a great deal in short order, you will be delighted by what you hold in your hand. It is a special gift not only to expound what the blessing of the triune God means, but also to explain why it matters. We have come to expect this from Derek Prime, and once again he hits the mark.'
ALISTAIR BEGG, SENIOR PASTOR, PARKSIDE CHURCH, CHAGRIN FALLS, OHIO

Seasons of comfort and joy

Meditations in verse based on
select Scritpure readings

ANNE STANDFIELD

96PP, PAPERBACK

ISBN 978-1-84625-103-0

God's Word, the Bible, is the guidebook
to life for all people. It is the 'measuring
rod' or standard by which we live out
our lives before God, the Creator of all
things. In it, God reveals himself to us
and teaches us about ourselves and the
world around us. God's Word is vital
in revealing the truth to each of us; only
the Bible teaches us how sinful people
can ever be reconciled to a holy God.

In these warm, Christ-centred poems,
Anne Standfield demonstrates her joy in
the truths of God's Word, sharing her
experiences of God and the knowledge
of his Word with others with a view that
they, with her, 'may know him better'
(Ephesians 1:17). All the poems have
been based solely upon Scripture with
the aim that each reader may come
to know the only true God and Jesus
Christ, his Son, whom he has sent as our
Saviour. This is the only way to eternal
life (John 17:3).

*Read some sample
poems on the
following pages*

Carried

[Based on Isaiah 46:3–5.]

O God of all strength,
    Who is like unto you?
He who bears us from birth
    And will carry us through;
He who shines in our darkness,
    Brings us hope in despair,
In whose arms we are resting;
    Who with you can compare?

Isaiah 46:4:
'… I have made you and I will carry you; I will sustain you and I will rescue you.'

Eternal mystery

[Based on Ephesians 1:7–14.]

Oh, the riches of God's grace,
    Lavished all on me,
In making known his wondrous plan—
    His eternal mystery!
For in the purpose of his will
    He chose me in his Son;
My heart now sings his glorious praise
    For all that he has done!

Ephesians 1:11–12:
'In him we were also chosen, having been predestined according to the plan of him who works out everything in conformity with the purpose of his will, in order that we, who were the first to hope in Christ, might be for the praise of his glory.'

Daystar

[Based on Revelation 22:16.]

The lengthening of days and the
    shortening of nights,
    Reversal of yonder celestial lights,
The day has arisen to show unto all
    Dominion of light over darkest nightfall.
God's Daystar arises within every heart
    To shine on forever, and ne'er to depart;
Sin's darkness he cleanses and evil dispels
    In every believer whose heart he indwells.

Revelation 22:16:
'I, Jesus … am the Root and the Offspring of David, and the bright Morning Star.'

Eternal Lamb

[Based on Isaiah 53:6.]

The eternal Lamb of God
    Has shed his precious blood
To bring the wanderers to the fold
    And lead us back to God.
So raise salvation's song
    To realms beyond the sky;
For God's own Son has sacrificed
    His life, that sin may die!

Isaiah 53:6:
'We all, like sheep, have gone astray, each of us has turned to his own way; and the Lord has laid on him the iniquity of us all.'

Unless

[Based on Matthew 7:18, 20.]

Matthew 7:18, 20:
'A good tree cannot bear bad fruit, and a bad tree cannot bear good fruit … Thus, by their fruit you will recognize them.'

Unless we show how much we care
　To each and every one,
How can one know Christ's love is there
Within our hearts, unless we share
　　God's only Son?

Unless the love of Christ abides,
　And we his fruit can see,
How can we know that one has cried
Unto the Lord, the crucified,
　　And been made free?

Unless we love as Christ has loved,
　How can one simply know
That Christ indwells us from above?
That we are filled with heavenly love?
　　Unless we show?

Unless that love of Christ is shown,
　How does one know there's care?
How does one know love's been made known
To those who say Christ's Name they own
　　Unless they share?

Steal not tomorrow

[Based on Psalm 31:14–15.]

*Psalm
31:14–15:*
*'But I trust in
you, O Lord; I
say, "You are
my God." My
times are in
your hands …'*

Steal not tomorrow out of the Father's hand,
For the time has not yet come to fulfil what he has planned;
Those moments are as precious as the many hours that pass,
But rest assured that, in his time, the answer comes at last.

God answers every prayer that a repentant sinner prays,
Yet it may not be the answer of our own desired way;
Sometimes it comes as 'No', and very often, 'Wait',
But no prayer goes unanswered that a true believer makes.

The precious school of patience he has called you to attend
To teach you there the meaning of an even better end.
He has not left you to endure without a cause in sight,
He knows that, by your waiting, you will learn his way is right.

And when that time has come when tomorrow is today,
And the answer's been revealed in the most diverse of ways,
Just thank the precious Father that he's ended all your sorrow
And spare a thought for someone who is praying for tomorrow.